ADAM'S DREAM

ADAM'S DREAM

POEMS

John J. Herman

New York

Copyright © 2024 John J. Herman

ISBN 978-1-956474-49-7

ISBN 978-1-956474-48-0 eBook

All rights reserved. No part of this book may be reproduced or transmitted in any form or by any means, electronic or mechanical, including photocopying, recording or by an information storage or retrieval system now known or heretoafter invented—except by a reviewer who may quote brief passages in a review to be printed in a magazine or newspaper—without permission in writing from the publisher: heliotropebooks@gmail.com

Cover artwork and design by Ronnie Ann Herman
Type design by Ronnie Ann Herman

THIS BOOK IS FOR MY DAUGHTERS

"The Imagination may be compared to Adam's dream—he awoke and found it truth."
                                        —Keats

CONTENTS

1 *TAKE UP*

BOOK ONE

5 LIFE ENDS WHERE IT BEGAN
6 OUSIA
7 SONG
8 PRAYER
9 TRAJECTORY
10 small
11 GNOSTIC
12 FOR SIMONE
13 BUTTERFLY
14 *Shells along the wall*
15 IT COMES AGAIN
17 HUNDREDS OF CHILDREN
18 TEA
19 THUMBS DOWN
20 COOLING
21 FOR DAVID
22 MORNING
23 THE FAMILIAR WAY
24 LINES
25 SAYING
26 FULLNESS
27 WHAT HE KNOWS

BOOK TWO

31 *TE DEUM*
32 THE ANIMALS LIVE CLOSE TO HEAVEN
33 HOW THE CLOUDS PASS
34 SPOT OF LIGHT

35 SHORTS
36 CURE
37 TO THE BONE
39 HURLED
40 THE POEM
41 A DANCE FOR BILL HERMAN
42 TWO
44 DISAPPOINTMENT
45 *Rain collects in drains, in pools, in crannies*
46 *I saw the world is made of sparks of light*
47 BEFORE AND AFTER
48 LOVE/WISDOM
51 NUNC STANS
52 POETRY
53 ROOTED
54 THE LAND OF BLANKNESS
56 *Things that are thrown away—old broken bricks*
57 SHORTS
58 THE POET
59 *What reaches out to touch the living flesh*
61 *Where*
62 *As when*
63 BECAUSE OF THE QUIET
65 DAYS
66 *It is the particular, is the single rose*
67 THROUGH A GLASS
68 *Words cannot say the Green that is the World*
69 CLIMB UPWARD, POET
70 LIGHT IN DARKNESS
71 *Because that beauty slipped between your hands*

BOOK THREE

75 I *We fill up the sky*
77 II *Adam dreamt the world*
78 III *Eve was everything that Adam loved*
79 IV *Sun lay on her beaches*

80 V *Adam's dream was cause*
82 VI *Adam said Yes to Eve*
83 VII *Adam dreamt the World*

<u>BOOK FOUR</u>

87 AUGUST
88 THE MUSIC OF SUMMER
89 THIS CADENCE THAT I BEAT
90 AFRAID OF THE NIGHT
91 *At night it is the pain*
92 WRATH
93 SHORTS
94 GENERATIONS
95 SWEET SIXTEEN
96 EVENING
97 INSIDE
98 PROVINCIAL
99 HOW LIGHT IS LIKE THE MIND OF GOD
100 THE CRYSTAL SPHERE
101 OTHERS
103 SIMPLE
104 THE BLOOD OF THE ROSE
105 *I know we all mythologize our women*
106 FAST
107 MY SISTER, LIFE
108 WIVES
109 MEXICO
110 DIRECTION
111 TRANSCENDENCE
112 FALLING
113 CLIMB!

<u>BOOK FIVE</u>

117 THE CALLING
119 *My father, my dear dead!*

120 FOR GABRIEL ON HIS SIXTEENTH BIRTHDAY
121 IF I DECLARE
122 TO THE LIGHTHOUSE
124 A RING A JEWEL A POT OF GOLD
125 BE AT EASE, BE SURE
126 LIKE CATTLE IN A FIELD
128 MOTETS
130 ANY DIETY
131 IF YOU COME THIS FAR
133 *Luminous, the flowers shine in light*
134 NOW THE BREATH OF THE WOMAN YOU LOVE
135 TITIAN WOULD HAVE PAINTED HER
136 DIVINING
137 UPON THE EARTH
139 *Because the loveliness of all this world*
140 THE STAGE
141 LABYRINTH
142 THE CIRCLE
143 THE TRADITION
144 SHORTS
146 *Whatever time has done, I love you more*
147 THE STAYING THINGS
149 ALWAYS A GIRL
150 *This ecstasy, this long drawn otherness*

153 Author Biography

TAKE UP...

You see your shadow where the sunlight falls,
The blank walls lit by the sun. And the leaves
Turn silver where they run—a thousand leaves
Running. And shadows stir, and darkness moves
Upon the face of the waters. This instant lies
Before you on the table . . . Take up
This hand, this instant, this word . . . Take up your life!

BOOK ONE

LIFE ENDS WHERE IT BEGAN

The same beeches, the same sycamores,
                    the identical odors,
with the aroma of chestnuts filling the avenue ....

Life ends where it began, colors,
                    the dresses of women,
noises, familiar voices, repeating

                    forward, forward!

OUSIA

Now
out of the breaking waves
the voice of the ocean
repeating
ousia, ousia—
you hear again
the syllables
in a language
before speech, there
where you lie
with the sting of salt
in your eyes
and the hiss and suck
of the sea
saying
in everlasting incantation
Being
Being
beneath
the black skin
of the waves.

SONG

There at the edge of the pit
Where depth goes down to fire
A cloud the shape of a rose
A rose the shape of desire.

A rose a cloud a word
And short time stretching between
Dark water in a stream
Holding the banks apart.

Along a city block
Count, now fast now slow,
Memory and the clock
Have locked the garden lock.

There at the pit's steep edge
Where fire eats like disease,
Go at peril, go at ease,
There, where the roses blow.

PRAYER

The world falls down around you
like broken glass. But why
the abysmal odor of mortality?

Pray to the flowers, pray to the gravel,
pray to the things that cannot possibly answer.

TRAJECTORY

There are names, there are faces,
there are familiar places
in a mythological landscape, as when
you turn, and suddenly
you are in Paris, in Paris sunlight,
in California, in California rain,
the identical transfigured
into another key—so many beads
strung on a string . . .
so many heads.
                    And you ask,
what did you hold, with summer
under the window, with traffic
under the window,
with evening
gilding the autumn leaves?
                    It was, of course,
the imperfect, the everyday,
a direction you chose, a way
you had to be—as when
you follow the trajectory
of a stone, its flight
rising in the grace
of the parabola,
until it curves,
it crests,
it falls . . . .

small

How small this life, barely a walnut shell!
Yet in the interstices, cities peoples worlds
forming and disforming. And the colors,
cobalt, magenta, sienna; the odors,
wax, bourbon, bread, and (if I may)
the odor of the woman you love . . .

Believe in small things, as a man
believes in sunlight, a flower,
a handful of shells. Believe
in simple words, as in Greek,
thanatos, agathos, aristoi—
the eternal language of tragedy.

GNOSTIC

One day the earth ate the sun—
and here we stand,

O fire! O flower!

Beads of light
at the edge of darkness,

with angels trafficking!

The air
is where we drown.

Look, look! Stars
plummet from the sky

like incandescent words!

FOR SIMONE

What now steps forth as from the water's depth,
The water lily, the flower, the young girl,
Whose features are in part my own, the weft
That is my daughter's—and as well my own.
I can watch history in this way unfurl
The light, the shining breadth, the denouement
Of this and that, of this *and* that, the pearl
That hung around the young girl's neck, the fount
Of generation, given to fashion this
Beauty that shines in darkness, radiance
Made out of darkness, which no longer is
Mere metaphor, but is the living dance

You dance upon the shore, below the home,
When deepest summer dwells in every bone.

BUTTERFLY

Mere zag of air, mere flitter of our sight,
You are yourself the petals that you grace;
You are yourself the air, whose steps you trace
With zigzag motion to the left and right
Until you settle on another stalk
To drink your fill of color from the source.
Your silence is your motion and discourse,
Your multicolored meaning is such talk
As you express in movement and in rest.
O syllable of wings that flutter so,
They speak in gesture, and the way they go
Makes visible the roads that they invest.
Your movement is the station of your being,
You are the pure embodiment of seeing!

Shells along the wall

Shells along the wall,
sand, and the seawall
where the breakers
rise, lifting the hair
of the waves. And
the horizon hisses
like a desert where
bells deliquesce,
with cords and bushels
by the ivory saddles,
and sandals
where you stand
in the bone-white
heat that bites
like salt
with odor of thyme
passing
like notes of
absence
that rise
that rise
into the air.

IT COMES AGAIN

White Summer, you come again,
but only like a letter
left in a drawer. August heat
under the collar,
the odor of farmyards, of cows,
the profusion of daisies
like simple words;
the fortuitous encounter
of sound and meaning, like
the good luck of the diver
plunging through air . . .

An unmowed field,
a narrow path . . . the
two of you
waiting by the stream,
you heavy with child,
the scent of water
fragrant in your hair.
                    What nights
with baby in the farther room,
with moonlight
crackling in the branches, with
August tangled in the trees . . .

                    White Summer,
you come again!
The sundrenched table
where you worked, the bees

blundering against the window;
poppies in a vermilion blaze,
the blue haze of forget-me-nots
crowding the wall—the
endless light
pouring over the patio,
like water from a bucket!

HUNDREDS OF CHILDREN

An aqueduct carried water to ancient Rome—
You saw it in Italy across the sun-filled landscape.

In Caesaria, city of Herod, King of the Jews, you saw
An aqueduct that had been built by the Roman legions,

The names of the legionnaires were scratched in the stone.
In Italy you climbed the aqueduct until you saw

The sun-burnt landscape below you. Your daughters
Ran across the top of the aqueduct, laughing.

Your head spun round. Hundreds of children
Were running across the aqueduct, you saw them

Running and laughing across the top of the aqueduct,
Far above the burnt-up landscape of Italy.

TEA

Taking tea in late afternoon
Was one of the things my mother favored most—
Her tea utensils out, her china cups,
Her strainer with its little swinging sieve
To catch the tea leaves in—with perhaps
A slice of buttered toast. O, happy times!
When Mother served me tea and sugar cubes,
And a plate of macaroons,
And we would sit and talk and laugh a bit,
And tea was fragrant as peppermint,
And Mother was only—well, let's see!
When Mother was only forty-two or three!

THUMBS DOWN

Thumbs down, and it is winter,
And it is Wisconsin, in Ice Station Zebra,
In zero degrees Fahrenheit beyond the window.

You are in the kitchen, you are drinking bourbon
With your father—and he says,
I am allowed one drink, they say it is good for me,

While outside the ice cracks
Like the knuckles of a convict.
You are inside, you are twenty-six,

You know your father can never die.

COOLING

After my father died, my mother

lay on the hospital bed beside him.

She held him, and she felt his body

cooling. *No quiero verla.* Your heart

cooled too, my mother,

the heart of my dear mother,

the cooling heart of my dear mother.

FOR DAVID

Gone forever, Brother, lost in the fits of life!
As if mere living should cause such grieving! David!
Sweet Singer of Israel. It is I who call you, your
Proper lover, loving as a brother—forever,
As the sun burns Being out of Nothing.

MORNING
For Peter

Now and at all times I can hear
Our mother moving in the farther room,
In the kitchen, in early morning,
At waking hour, in our childhood,
Like springtime in an apple tree.

The knock of pans, the rush of water,
The odor of breakfast, of percolating coffee,
The morning music on the radio—
A floating plantation of associations
Foreign, and inexpungibly familiar . . .

What word, what image, what illumination
In the backward recesses of memory?
Morning sounds, the fragrance of coffee,
The recurrent certainty of happiness—
Our mother moving in the farther room.

THE FAMILIAR WAY

There stands a door,
And, behind the door,
Another door, a path
Leading across the grass
Where we two would go
Daily, hand in hand,
Where the flowers stand,
Although it's also true
One often hears
Anger, shouting, tears,
Terror, fright,
A small voice in the night,
Love, the dirtied word—
All of that is heard,
Or nothing at all,
Only a dirty wall
Stained a wretched gray—
No other way,
Only the familiar way.

LINES

For him a tree was always a tree, a woman
The body of a woman. The world hurt him
With the impact of the particular, as when
The eye careens into an obstacle, and the conjunction
Abuts in the absolute of shock. It hurt him
With the impact of winter, as when the sky assumes
      the attributes of gray,
And snow falls hard and hard. It was also
Summer, with the syrup of summer, as in
The honeysuckle of childhood, the sun in its luxuriance,
The apple beyond one's reach. But if it was childhood,
It was only the apparition of childhood in its otherness, the
Inescapable projection of the present into a location
Where winter is the memory of winter, summer
The sense of summer in its abstract habitation. So
August was a succession of Augusts, real finally
In the dimension of memory, a place more spacious
Than the this-or-that: the place you would inhabit—
      if you could.

SAYING

For Nathan

My little boy, how difficult to say
Love-for-a-child. How quickly used-up words
Get used! The penchant runs astray
Into the dialect of the already-heard,

Already used before too many times,
All chewed and masticated, till it's like
A poet's masticated, chewed-up rhymes
That clap and clatter—speech without a bite,

Papier-mâché! Not the living stuff
Of respiration, exfoliation
Into the outer leaf of such and such,
Reality, actuality, expression.

Nor is it true that silence is the word
To say our love, whose presence speaks its name
As clear as silence can, and is referred
Out of silence into the living flame

That shapes our speaking tongue. So, once begun,
The word of love will find its breathing way
Into the world of Love, whose currents run
Into the voice of speech, which then can say.

FULLNESS

The fullness of green is what the eye can see;
It puffs the trees, it fluffs the bushy leaves;
Nor is it what the mind alone perceives,
But existentially *so*, the power to *be*.

Let's call it the miracle exoteric,
The Oroboros that can bite its tail,
Greenest summer filling out its sail,
Then disappearing like a candlewick.

The Fullness of Time is something else entire,
The mystic vision of transcendent air
That is not here and yet is everywhere,
Consuming earth in esoteric fire.

Between the two the World is rounded Being,
Both what we see and what we are not seeing.

WHAT HE KNOWS

He knows the sun. He knows the wind that's heard
Beating the bushes like a child's stick;
He knows the moon by sight alone, just like
A beauty passing by without a word.

Darkness he knows, which is the rounded dark
Where stars appear, and the tripartite moon,
And summer weather with its green that soon
Turns red, turns bronze, turns brown as peeling bark.

He knows the tug and tension of his breath
Huffing and puffing in right utterance;
Yet utterance itself makes little sense;
He is foreclosed, he cannot know his death.

He knows the kingdom that is his to keep
Only the briefest while, twixt sleep and sleep.

BOOK TWO

TE DEUM
For R.

The garnet in the ring, the nettle in the flower,
the word in the sentence that stings . . . Stand now
in the dark inspiration of light, not knowing
your name, your father's name, your brother's, for
there is no other, no, not any—although your life

was sworn to that constancy. *Te Deum!*
Words cannot say *I love*, as they cannot say *Farewell.*
The daughter who disappeared, the sentences you conceived,
are inscribed in a cadence of a different measure,
sonatas in the syllables of silence . . . We must

pledge ourselves to the music, like
the flowers in Italy that romped beside us
by the masonry, where for an instant we stood,
with the rainbow burning above us, and the road
ran onward into eternity—darkness into light,

light into the inspiration of darkness.

THE ANIMALS LIVE CLOSE TO HEAVEN

The animals live close to Heaven.
Their noses know its scent,
Their eyes pressed tight to the glass
Like fingers to a ball. Men
Live at sixes and sevens,
Their breath a stench,
Their minds a clever snarl.

Sad words, sad truth
At end of swirling day,
Where tongue for lack of praise
Saddens, and wisdom
Cracks like a tooth. Raise
A paean, Carpenter, if you can,
To the broken wisdom of man,

Who stands outside the gate
To temporize, to expatiate,
Although the day be short, the hour late,
And in the western skies reverberate
The dyings of another day,
The weight of too much wait,
And nowhere close to Heaven.

HOW THE CLOUDS PASS

The knight lies in the grass

The maiden weeps beside him

Tears form on the face of the day

On the grass of the meadow

On the long shadows of afternoon

Where the horse grazes in a field

Although the clouds keep passing over

Like blind eyeballs, insisting

That nothing has happened

SPOT OF LIGHT

O spot of light, brilliant place of being!
Genius and effective source of seeing,
Scion of the sun, whose genius is
The power and the force of genesis.
See how you lie as quiet as a wing
A butterfly will trill without moving,
A thought that hovers, inspiration of
All movement, though itself does never move.
True philosopher of the inner eye,
Whose sight is insight of transparency,
Listen to nothing, harken to no sound
That issues from the voices that abound
Of our mortality, of the passing day;
Be the silence of eternity
Made visible, made palpable to sight,
Be the living nerve-end of insight.

SHORTS

i

Pitiful—or less than pitiful,
It makes no difference at all.
Drink whatever you will,
You're sure to get your fill.

ii

Sobriety, piety, gravitas,
Such the trinity
For this poor pain-in-the ass.

iii

Run as fast as you can,
Ambitious little man,
The only race to run
Is the one you're running on.

iv

Though serious emotions run rife
From beginning to the end of life,
Most serious men agree,
Life's not to be taken too seriously.

CURE

The heart fills up with bile,
The arteries with grease,
What's the cure for these?
What the known release?

Well, the known release
Is worse than the disease,
And consists of this,
An overdose of death.

TO THE BONE
For my daughers

You cut yourself to the bone . . .

And the sun streamed through the window—
how many years ago?

The small hand lay on the pillow,
it was the hand of the child . . .

I have not said all I have to say.

It was the head of an otter
swimming . . . *Being*, I say,

comes out of Nothing,
ex nihilo . . . (I have said this before) . . .

but the words *are* the poem,
they rise up like startled birds,

they are your own . . .
Say the things that vanish,

the gold fold of the leaf. The tears,
the unextinguishable tears . . . Say

the accumulation of a lifetime . . .
(But have you thanked enough

those who helped you? Those
who reach out to help? Have you thanked

the dead?) . . . And the small voice
sang in the grass . . .

(World without end!)

*I have not said
all I have to say—*

end without end! Give

whatever you have,
the gold tip of the leaf.

*(And my ending is despair
unless I be released by prayer)* . . .

The small hand lay in your hand,

and the edge of the knife
cut to the bone.

HURLED

Greening, now filling out the world
Into its fire of green, in which we're hurled
Joyfully, hopefully, burningly, as when
The youthful poet reaches for a pen,
And all is music—as we hope to be,
If all is consummated mercifully,
Although we don't deserve such consummation,
Dancing in greenness in exfoliation,
Like the greening budding springtime world,
Into which like stones we've all been hurled.

THE POEM

Slowly the Poem accumulates,
a cycle of spring and winter,
a succession of names and places,
of tears and mucus and babies.
The eye makes love to the world,
while overhead the sky
shoots like glass. This is the Poem,
the accretion of rings
as in a redwood. We
thicken like sclerosis:
thought into dogma,
inspiration into repetition,
insight into ideology . . . but
the Poem persists, it
gathers to its perfection
of imperfection,
it sings
like a chorus of boys,
it lies down in your arms.
It whispers like a gentian, it whirs
like a spinning wheel—
it fills up the world.

A DANCE FOR BILL HERMAN
For Joanna

I recall you're dancing at the French restaurant,
Astounding the young waitress with your pranks!
Now twisting *en arriere*, now *en avant*—
And that alone deserves our warmest thanks!
Transforming life into transparent play,
Transforming it by means of your own wit—
Beyond whatever bodily decay
At eighty-seven years, might hinder it.
And then I think of how you loved Joanna,
As if the love of body could not age!
The love of spirit, with its own hosanna
Of secular delight, whatever it presage.

And then I count up loss, and how much less
We all now are, without your gay *sagesse*.

TWO

    i

Can these stones
speak? Can these bones
be silent? For
the ocean repeats I Am,
you hear it
over and over,
where the dunes
abut the sea—
the eternal voice
speaking its name,
like stars
bejeweling the sky—
a promise
unnoticed—but not
a promise withheld.

    ii

In the peculiar
contrariety
of yourself
and the Other,
it is the Other
by which we know. What
can be forgotten?
not even a sparrow! Behold
the dead
moving in silence,
moving in otherness,

like stars that shine above us
in perpetuity!

DISAPPOINTMENT

Let us now sing
our disappointment, who once
was our daughter dancing. Let us
praise the light, the stones,
the overarching sky,
which God made,
not man... Who taught *you*
to sing to swim to dance
the turn and counterturn,
you agon! You atom
from a smoking candle... You
danger, you daughter,
you disappearing.

Rain collects in drains, in pools, in crannies

Rain collects in drains, in pools, in crannies
Of the heart, you hear it sloshing,
Clogging the carburetor. It loses power,
That celebrated organ, it barely
Makes the grade. And what of you, my girl?
So distant, you are but a sound
Far out at sea. And there you remain,
Dwindling like Icarian smoke—like candles
At your Birthday Party—which
Never happened, right? . . . What monster
Haunts the corridors where you wander?
What darkness? What flibbertigibbet? . . .
Light returns—but not for us, my daughter,
My onetime commandment. The engine
Won't start. The motor is flooded. The tires
Spin in the mud . . . Stagnant water clogs the heart.

I saw the world was made of sparks of light

I saw the world was made of sparks of light
That dance and weave within the hemisphere,
And all of them—now white, now blue—appear
Like gleaming gems within the gathering night
That harbors all. And they are marvelous,
And they are frightening; for they will dance,
Then—disappear!—never to return. A glance
Suffices, and they're gone, although the source
Of all their pin-point dancing never dies,
But, quick as thought, replenishes to full
The space with newborn sparks, in prodigal
Refreshment. So are furnished ever new supplies
Of sparks that soar where others just have been,
Then disappear, and nevermore are seen.

BEFORE AND AFTER

It is a kind of cosmic joke, I guess,
That we, like ants, must scurry in this quarter,
A dot in cosmic space, a mere backwater,
A most unwelcomed, most unlikely guest,
Whose tireless mind, whose quick imagination
Peoples the void with legends of its own,
As if this Nothing were in fact a home
Concocted for our pleasured satisfaction,
A warmth that circles round us like a dove
Bringing messages from afar,
Saying that God is Love, so that we are
Snug in our cosmic hutch, watched from above.

And yet for sure it is no laughing matter,
The Nothingness that comes before and after.

LOVE /WISDOM
For N.

     i

The eye beholds
the world of apples.
It beholds
sunlight on a stone,
laundry drying,
a wedding, a cancer,
a baby crying.

The eye
describes a vase,
a planted tree;
understands
what man has made
by hand,
a wall, a home—not
earth, the dome
of stars,
a shining piece of stone.

     ii

The Ganges—
mystic river
of time
and excrement... people
the color of mud
till the fields... heat,
slime, a dance

of men and women,
a hut, a child
washed into the sea,
washed
like laundry
into the sea.

    iii
Buddha
sees eternity,
he sees
nor bud nor tree
nor sad humanity,
sees
neither hand
nor land
nor shriveled apple
lying in the grass.

Neither face
nor place
nor child departing;
only emptiness,
the subsumption
of all particulars
into
unbecoming—
undirtied
by love—not
desire
but fire,

the World turning,
the World burning
forever,
root
and
branch
and truth—

and
Truth

NUNC STANS

August, like a door that slams . . .
a voice, a noise, the sudden uproar
of far-off thunder. And you recall
the earth beneath you shifting,
in San Francisco, as you lay
beside your love,
twenty stories above the ground.
It comes again, the fire,
the apocalypse, the quotidian—although
you will not come again . . . Summer
slams the door, a god
violent or serene or indifferent.
It is a window that opens
onto a meadow, onto two daughters
dancing—the *nunc stans*
of the immovable, always departing,
irreplaceable Now.

POETRY

It comes again,
the wave

that is your own,
as when young women

dance in a ring,
their bodies swaying—you

cannot take your eyes away!
again, again—

against all likelihood,
rejoicing!

ROOTED

Rooted in the ground,
a bush, a rock, a tree,
an animal, a man,
an upright you, a me,
speaking the truth
as best we can,
since truth must be
spoken, the she, the he,
the hurt, the need,
since human beings die,
must disappear, so we
must try
to be
rooted,
as bush, as tree,
as possibility!

THE LAND OF BLANKNESS

You come at last to the land of blankness.
The trees are dust, mere skeletons of dust,
The colors a dusty gray—not red, not green,
But only the likeness of blank sleep. You look to fields,
Less fields than mere extension, a rhetoric
Without communication, an endless blab.

How did you discover this pit of gravel,
This sunless, this pointless attenuation?
This looks to be reality, the actual
Reduced to desiccation, stale inspiration,
A weariness that makes of life
A redacted memory, a long regret.

At every road you step into the landscape
Of unbelief, into the dried up place
Of closed-in space, within the kingdom
Of dried grass, white sun, stale scent,
Where once the windrows flourished,
Filling the thankful sense with summer air.

The sky sits close upon you like old age.
What entrance, what transit, what exit?
What meaning in this place of meaningless distance
Where you cross and cross with thirst upon your tongue?
This life that throbs like thought without an object?
This endless trek of feet across a plain?

Small breeze at evening rustles the hills.
Sun melts like gold in the uncut grass.
You peer into a well of bottomless dimension
Where sounds remind you hauntingly of laughter.
Out of the depthless dark there rises sound
That brings the taste and smell of distant laughter.

Things that are thrown away—old broken bricks

Things that are thrown away—old broken bricks
Left from a bookshelf, a dull paring knife,
Embroidery belonging to your wife
When she was young, rag dolls, pick-up sticks—
Toys the girls would play with, your mother's pin . . .
Your mother. Photographs never taken
Save by the fading brain. Mistaken
Ambitions from a game you couldn't win,
Or never cared to play . . . What did you play?
Husband brother father son . . . Exhaustion
From races that you ran, or didn't run,
Handfuls of confetti, handfuls of dry hay,

Handfuls of clay still warm, or otherwise,
Cooling in ovens where the bread won't rise.

SHORTS

i

The thickness of the darkened air
Spreads persuasion everywhere
That the final shade shall give
Darkness its right privilege.

ii

What is the cry the bleeding heart emits?
What the need of our poor human wits?
To be, to be!—kinetic or in stasis,
Not the fabled Reason of noesis.

iii

The agate ring that winks like Odin's eye,
A tuft of grass beside the railroad tie—
Such are the objects that define what is,
The poem itself in mind's quick genesis.

iv

What can be said in prose, in poetry,
Are different in kind as in degree:
For one is limited by the rational mind,
The other by infinity.

THE POET

What can we say of Shelley, whose poor girls
Suffered so terribly from his high-strung nerves?
His Poet's nerves, I mean to say, the true
Expression of the poet's (*entre nous*)
Proclivity for beauty, his rash fate
To have his cake and also eat his cake.
Shelley, alas, is what the poet *is*,
A true type of the scholar's nemesis,
Whom the bourgeois mind prefers to know
Only so far as printed page can go,
Wagging its finger at the very thing
That makes the poet *be*, that makes him sing!

What reaches out to touch the living flesh

What reaches out to touch the living flesh
lives in the flesh—a breathing testament
of hand of mouth of voice of faithful name.

Such is the lexicon of lost communication
articulated daily by the passing air,
the tradition, the connection, the handing on,

the handing down, as a box is handed
down to a younger brother under the ladder,
under the attic, under the small trap door

through which each living person has
(we're told) an entrance to the Mind of God,
his private hidden doorway of the self.

So Emerson, that strange uncanny man,
whose younger brother died, the same as mine,
who stood behind me on the living stair.

What reaches out to touch the living flesh,
a long-lost voice, a much loved name, a sound,
lives in the mind as its own testament,

a traveled way, a road, an unclasped door
which opens onto meadows, onto seas,
onto a field of flowers, onto God,

onto the death that stands beneath the door
holding the ladder as a brother might,
a hand, a right connection, a true voice.

Where

the snap of day?
clouds
strung out in sentences?
leaves
in exuberant exfoliation,
the wind-
flecked sea, the dew
diamond-scintillant? Where
girls with
cool-blown breezes
tight as silk
against their thighs?

Summer,
the polyphonous,
transposes death
to apples. It brings
the sweep of wind,
the heat of sun,
the thunder crack
of rain. It brings
the short long days
that hold
the hornet's
quick incision,
the cicada's gibber,
the philosopher,
the sorcerer,
the poet.

As when

flowers are beaten to the ground,
their heads
hang like birds
painted by a seventeenth century master
commemorating death; so
the daisies on the lawn—
God's flags,
are beaten by the rain
until their heads
lie
like the heads of birds
stricken
to the ground.

BECAUSE OF THE QUIET
For Asher

There is an old man, he is trying to say
"I love you." It is your grandfather, he has long been dead,
he is trying to reach you across the distance,

trying to say these words, the accumulation of generations.
You are embarrassed, you turn aside,
being a child, being an eight-year old,

not understanding, not wishing to understand
such simple communication. But the clouds
pass over with the same simplicity,

they cast their shadows on the hills, they say,
you too were here, you too were once a boy,
you too impressed your footsteps on the grass.

The small hand that you held, the larger hand,
the hand of the eight-year old—it is the hand
of your grandson, the hand of your daughter,

the hand of your father as he held your hand,
yourself an eight-year old, the world an adventure,
a dream of sound and sight and flashing color,

as fields of sun flare with the white of grass,
though you won't see the fields again—although
you recall them on your tongue, your eye . . .

But will the child?—as the mouth remembers
sweetness in summer, the hand the force of a ball... For
there is only remembrance, there is only the calling back,

as the mother called at evening from the window,
the old man from the dead now calls the child,
the grandchild, the loved one, the always remembered,

because of the quiet, because of the stillness, because of the forgetting.

DAYS

That day
we lay
at ease
in the Pyrenees;

and the rain
hard
on the pane,
on the boulevard;

the season
in the Caribbean
with seas
and mangrove trees;

the sound
of the city
gritty
and unsound;

day by day
eaten away!
How can this be?
You, me—

eternity!

It is the particular, is the single rose

It is the particular, is the single rose,
The ant that labors by the paving stone,
The single woman waiting in the room,
The daughter in the garden in the light.

Voices, incidents, a ladder in a barn,
A stair, a rocking chair, a silver spoon:
These things that served their purpose, spoke their name,
Uttered their sentence and then disappeared.

The wind above the shore makes ocean sounds,
The clouds turn upward like the thoughts of men,
The birds, turned evanescent in the blue,
Deliquesce like men, and disappear.

THROUGH A GLASS

You see the summer backward in a glass,

as if death were opinion only. You see

the truth as through an old man's glasses:

the bay in Maine, the headland, the dark seals,

the folding white of waves, the plash of oars . . .

What glass, what sea, what fragments of a day?

Ocean, salt, childhood, sliding sails,

A cove, a wind-swept tree . . . the certainty of death.

Words cannot say the Green that is the world

Words cannot say the Green that is the world,
Though green shout out its name like summer weather;
The truth of things is hidden to discover
How hard it is to find the fitting word!
Green is not leaf, it is not grass or sky
Or flesh or death. It clothes the breathing earth
In absolute; and though we may rehearse
Its vast particulars, and multiply
The instances of green, they are not Green,
Which is in truth a transcendental fire.
We must, if we would catch it live, aspire
To something higher, something that's not seen
Except by the seeing mind, which then can see
Green in its living Universality.

CLIMB UPWARD, POET

Climb upward, poet, till you see
The world in its vast symmetry
Curving beneath in groves and fields
Like the sight the ocean yields
When the sun beats on the waves
In sparkling points, in darting rays,
Ordering in rows the eye to see
The marvel of such majesty!
Thus Nature with its arts will set
Throughout, its living alphabet,
Behind which dwells the final Source,
Ultima Thule's true discourse.

LIGHT IN DARKNESS

i

I do not have to know the depth of things
If I'm allowed only to see their face,
For certainly the face itself is grace
Enough, without depth's other imagings.

ii

How does it happen, what the hidden reason,
Man is cast down from season unto season?
What the Law, what the unaltered Way,
From dawn to dusk, from dusk to break of day?

iii

Leaves, like the generations of men,
With the aid of their osmotic stem,
Suck up moisture from the earth, so when
One generation dies, another starts again.

iv

What is the Light in Darkness but the Dead?
They move in sable motion through the head,
Like Love, that comes unsummoned to the heart,
Offering tinder, so the fire may start.

Because that beauty slipped between your hands

Because that beauty slipped between your hands…
It was a flower, it was an unmowed field,
It was blond light that trilled against a wall.

It was all things in brightest complication
Falling away to Nothing—although it was
The certainty that such a thing can't be.

For there they stand—the sky in orange-green;
The zigzag crack across the frozen lake;
The wind against the headland whipping the trees.

Thus it must happen with all flashing things:
The *rien de tout* that spoke the abiding word—
The flaming leaf that burned upon the bough.

BOOK THREE

ADAM'S DREAM (I)

We fill up the sky, we fill it up
with what we see—as when
a son is gone, a mother
fills up his room with flowers.

We fill up the sky
with birds, with clouds, with distance,
and then
we fill it up again
with what we do not see—
invention, revelation,
intrusion, delusion:
a god,
a nothing.

The earth is filled with bones
and dirt—a rib
picked white as stone,
an apple on a bough,
a rose, a long goodbye,
a meeting round a fire,
a word, a myth... We fill it up

with what is there, and then
we fill it up again
with what is not,
an absence, an emptiness,
a nothing, a naught—
so that

when we awake and look around,
and see this world
of hurt and loveliness,

we know it is our own.

ADAM'S DREAM (II)

Adam dreamt the world. He dreamt the sun and stars,
The ripple of water and the crash of waves.
He dreamt the lightning and the bass of thunder,
The taste of honey and the odor of baked bread.
Adam dreamt the clouds that slowly pass,
Casting their shadows. He dreamt the multi-seasons
In their endless track across the mind. He dreamt
Eve, lovely as weather. When she touched him,
She gathered the world about them like a shawl.
She was the heat of sun and scent of rain,
The home to which he came at end of day.
Thus Adam dreamt the World, the generations
Passing in their interconnectedness. He dreamt
The wonder and the horror and the beauty,
And when he awoke, he saw that it was true.

ADAM'S DREAM (III)

Eve was everything that Adam loved,
Summer, apples ripened on a bough;
She was the space that stretched about him, so
The things he saw could name the things he knew,
The meanings he bestowed, the breathing word,
The weighted chord of sound, the apple's core.

The ring they gave betrothed them to the earth;
The golden circuit was their testament.
He would follow wheresoe'r Eve went,
Because of devotion, because of electric need,
As earth to sun, as child to his mother,
As one to one in breathing sacrament.

This was his dream, the truth that had been made
Out of his rib, out of his living side,
So that in sleep he'd see again, would touch
The otherness he loved, the shape, the warmth,
The words she uttered and the road she chose,
The arrow pointed at his panting heart.

ADAM'S DREAM (IV)

Sun lay on her beaches, wind stirred in her hair,
Meadows offered their summer throats of ease.
The apple gave its roundness and the peach
Its sweetness to assuage her eager tongue.
The eye ate Eve as, stepping forth, she took
The sea's soft sunlight onto her new-washed hair.
Her life became the myth of generations
Woven within the substance of the day;
Her mind the forest hills and floating clouds
That rode the bounding air above her head.
She became the gravity of the earth
And, gravely too, the grave in which men lie.
She is man's dream so that he's not alone
And lonely on this earth, which is his home.

ADAM'S DREAM (V)

Adam's dream was cause of blood and grief,
As back and forth he tossed in troubled sleep.
His groans awoke young Eve, who heard his cries

And lay her hand upon his heaving side,
Hoping to ease the terror and the dread
That hurt him so, and held him in their grasp.

So he awoke and stared at her, and she
Could see he did not know who lay beside him,
His only wife, the progress of his rib.

Slowly he found his breath. His large eyes gazed,
Seeing the slopes of gentle Eve, his wife;
He knew her then, and whispered her soft name.

Eve, he said, what is this terrible dream
That comes with darkness to destroy my sleep,
Seeming to speak of things we cannot know—

Knowledge of what's to come, a groaning world,
A tide of flesh and blood and broken faith,
Crushing the earth, crushing our future sons.

I saw a whirlwind of such men twist up,
Blown like a cataract, a chaos that had sprung
Up from the fearful earth to touch the sky

Like flame like wind like blood like molten stone.
And time itself lay tight embraced with death,
Mixed in that mess, which portioned out their death,

So that no human, woman man or child,
Woman in her grace, nor innocent child,
Escaped its share of that most sure destruction

That rampaged on the earth and scorched the sky,
Leaving its name deep burned into the flesh
Of all our offspring, all our heritage.

Eve in her fright stared at him hard, as if
His mind were touched, to make him speak like that,
Of fearful portends not to be believed,

As if her Adam did not know the truth
That God had told them of, that time they walked
In dew of the day together. For His words

Had promised love and gentleness to all
The creatures of the earth, especially man.
Now Adam too grew silent, for Eve's words

Had spoken more to him than Eve could know.
A double meaning grew up in his mind,
Which he would not divulge to gentle Eve.

But now he saw, and now he understood
The burden and the meaning of his dream,
As if from highest Pisgah he saw all.

ADAM'S DREAM (VI)

Adam said Yes to Eve, and so he fell—
For what is mortal is but passingness.
And love between the sexes is all well
And good, but mortal as the vessels that possess

That heady mixture. For we are told
(And I believe it true) that Nature itself
Is governed by Love, whose strong and manifold
Persuasion, guides and binds each budding sheaf

Of being, from atom unto gods. Adam
Said yes to mortal Eve, and so he chose
Mortality, our human destiny, from
Out Eternity, the Transcendental Rose.

For we are our nature, and our nature is
Party to Nature, not Transcendent Bliss.

ADAM'S DREAM (VII)

Adam dreamt the World—beginning, middle, end:
Existence, Judgment, and Apocalypse.
He dreamt the earth with its uncanny blend
Of sweet and blood, the rose leaf with its pricks

Tearing the flesh. We are its little men,
Who live our little lives only to die.
We disappear like smoke—but rise again
In different guise, like weeds or summer flies.

Yet we its cynosure, this object who
Scurries like ants across the narrow ground;
Its worshippers as well, with buffalo
Sketched upon the rock-face all around.

Such is Adam's dream, the world we know,
Into whose small dimensions we awake
To dream the sun, to dream time's ceaseless flow
That swirls about us, certain as mistake.

BOOK FOUR

AUGUST

August was much too short—just seventy years!
Just seventy Augusts with their length of sun,
Their sweep of wind, their sweet of honeycomb,
Their cry of crickets when the twilight nears—

Over before begun! We could not hold
(Although we knew it would not come again!)
The waters from the sluice that swiftly ran
Below the meadow, where the light turns gold.

It turns to memory, like the chrysalis,
From which the butterfly (like fluttering smoke)
Escapes into the air . . . and forms the yoke
Of sunlight's yellow setting, whose emphasis

Brings in the night. And so the western plain
Burns for the moment with the ore that spills
Over the broad horizon, till it fills
The gulf below with its own deeper stain.

The years fill up with darkness, like the sky,
Whose dark is only darker for the stars;
Their provenance is set so very far,
We could not hear them, even should they reply.

THE MUSIC OF SUMMER

Now that summer has come,
you taste again the music of summer.

You stumble, you stutter words,
as if there were a means to say

this excess: flowers, grass, trees....
Time is on fire, its flame

singes the rose. The weathered barn,
the bending elm, the handle of the pump

beaded in moisture: these are ways
to say the fullness that we breathe,

the here the now the there the always—
the recurrent music of summer.

THIS CADENCE THAT I BEAT

This cadence that I beat upon the ground,
This interval of words, this moving mesh,
How is it not the green grass that I thresh
To make into this offering of sound?

This sound of words and meaning and of time
That moves in dance-like rhythm to the eye,
As to the ear, as time in time sweeps by,
And we attain to syllable and rhyme;

And to the sweeping dance the mind must know
If it should know the step of any measure
Woven by man, to give the mind such pleasure
As mind is native to and time can show.

O, this the cadence that the poets know,
And beat with pleasure at their pleasured best,
To give the laboring mind its peck of rest,
And hold the dizzy mind and toe in tow.

AFRAID OF THE NIGHT

Afraid of the night!
How can I wash away
This imperishable clay
That smudges out the light?

The linear roads lead on
Like arrows, piercing the day;
They cannot turn away
From their trajectory.

Wisdom, where are you?—
Teach what we eschew,
Who fear the healing dark,
Which washes all anew.

And yet the gathering night
Moves strangely, like a shark
That ripples in the dark,
And feeds outside the light.

At night it is the pain

At night it is the pain of what has been
Troubles your sleep. I mean
The things that in the daytime seem unreal,
The so-called little things, the barely real,
Childhood failures, failures to those you love,
Failures of love itself, unlovely facts
Concerning things that were, the *that-which-was*—
The simple truth! O power, O mighty force,
Hurricane strength, fierce tidal wave, O, how
Be mindful for the little man, the every-day,
The errant acts, the quick dismissive words
Scripted across the pages of the absurd,
The multiplicity of possibility
That shatters certainty, that makes a joke
Of you, of me, of all we say we say,
The profligate complicity—the truth!
These things that shouldn't be and yet are so,
The one two three of truth's simplicity,
The bleeding fact, the wild hurt of the world!

WRATH

The powers that be, the gods,
Made suffering for man
So he might understand
By word or book or rod

The state that he is in,
Congenital, by Law,
And can, if fast or slow,
Set aside his sin

Through suffering, and win
Wisdom, or what at least
Conduces to such peace—
Patience to begin

The steep steps to the place
Above the mountain's height,
Which effort might excite
Mercy, and find grace.

SHORTS

i

Our penance is such,
Although we know too much,
We don't do as we should—
Payable in blood.

ii

The eye that only imitates reflection,
Can grant at best quotidian perception.

iii

Purgatorial flame
licks like rain
against the stone.

Thus by sure degree
and slow monotony—
filigree!

iv

Men and women come together
Like points of light in roughest weather,
So our mortal inclination
Gravitates to such election!

v

In the wrinkled form of love
It still is love that stamps above
The hardened earth. We wear boots
To plant love deeply to its roots.

GENERATIONS

Like stones on Easter Isle, the great dead stand
Staring fixedly out to farthest sea;
They look to distance, to the living land
Where mortals hug their own inadequacy.

The dead look out with such a steady gaze,
They count the fingers of great-grandchildren.
Earlier generations they can scan with ease—
Their reach is competent, their love is greatly given.

But our poor eyes can't pierce beyond our days:
We think the years outside our brief inspection,
Beyond the scope of our small intellection,
Are fictive stories, tales of fabled ways.

Unmindful of the love that binds us round—
Like light that shines through clouds, but without heat
Sufficient to the weather to confound
The frost that girds us in our small retreat—

We move in ignorance of the wealth bestowed,
Which to our weakling minds is but fool's gold.

SWEET SIXTEEN
For K.

Do you remember, in that summer heat,
We scoured the city to find you ice-cream cake?
It was your birthday celebration—Sweet
Sixteen! I'd promised sweets for your sweet sake,
Prosecco for your friends—glasses of it!
And ice cream cake—a special birthday dish
Not easily procured! You'd forfeit it,
You said—but I replied, *No way!* It was the wish
You fancied most—so in that sweltering heat
We searched for it until—at last!—we found
A Carvel shop that had your choice, replete
With your own name, and roses all around!

O Sweet Sixteen! and now so far away—
That long, that lost, that melted ice-cream day!

EVENING

Where night bears down upon the silent woods,
The forest odors rise into the nostrils:
Moss, dead leaves, needles from the pines.
The trees bisect the gathering forms of night,
And silence spreads around us without bourne.
Aristotle believed that God can neither know
Nor love created things, but broods eternally
Upon Himself, the Unmoved Mover of the All.
Perhaps that's why we are ourselves so lonely,
So centered on the me, the paltry *I*,
The forked and crooked, naked human self.
Night descends like thunder to the deaf,
Filling the dark declivity of earth. A quiet
Past understanding, an absolute:
The darkening man, the fast departing sun.

INSIDE

The boy can feel his death stirring inside,
Like roots beneath the earth. Without the light,
The stems within that depth grow ghostly white,
Bereft of chlorophyll, whose force has dyed
The outer leaves to green. He feels death move,
Like an animal deep within its burrow;
His instincts sense the tiny, seismic echo
Shivering up to him. Nothing can remove
The earthquake that will follow. This is death,
Waxing inside him like another life.
(So it happens when a young pregnant wife
Feels the stirring deep inside of her.) But this breath
Foretells an end approaching without sound,
That then shall rip up roots, and split the ground.

PROVINCIAL

This is the corner of the world
that is your own, the provincial,
the only one you'll ever see. It is
the universal algebra that gathers
all particulars: snowfall
over the Catskills; sunlight
on the Atlantic; the
Parisian *arrondissement*
darkened in rain.

Here is the familiar
collected in its peculiarity:
the twisting staircase, the dusty lane
running to town; a circle
that is your private eye,
repeated like birdsong, like syllables
in a nursery rhyme: an opportunity,
a necessity,
a way of knowing,
a way of saying your name.

HOW LIGHT IS LIKE THE MIND OF GOD

                i

How is light like the Mind of God?
Invisible, yet changing all to sight,
So that, when any object's seen aright,
It offers vision of the Axelrod!

                ii

The Law is God Himself in his own Act
Creating and sustaining every day
The World, and the broad heavenly display
Of all the shining objects we call fact.

                iii

Light is like truth, which is too fine to know
Except derivatively, in the fast or slow
Expostulation of the committing Act
That God reveals as his right artifact.

THE CRYSTAL SPHERE

The marvel of the sky entices one
To ponder on its broad harmonium,
A shining jewel, a crystal sphere, and so
Competent to hold the things below
In its reflection—a design
In which the solid earth turns crystalline.
To think upon this steadily and see
The complex of its huge anatomy,
Purifies the mind, till it exalt
One's thoughts to imitate that shining vault,
Which holds the earth and stars and all things else
Easily, within its plenteous wealth,
And scatters gold like rain, though only on
Those whose sight can boldly look upon
The wonder of that ideal symmetry
Burning like fire for mortal eyes to see.

OTHERS

i

In the everyday
you stumble
you cry out
you fall...
It is the confusion
the satisfaction
the astonishment
of being
here, now,
this single instant,
this only time.

ii

Night,
and the brilliant
arc of the stars;
you look to see
a ship far out at sea,
flashing. It is
a beauty passing
in the dark,
a queen
trailing her phosphorescent silks
across the sky.

iii

Moon swell
and roses, and

the odor of night,
the bite
of the small-mouthed smile,
the unaccountable
attestation of the flowers—
the inexhaustible,
unceasing
exclamation,
Here!

    iv

Light is truth.
    We cross the Jordan
hand in hand, entering
the Promised Land,
    singing....

Dark is truth.
    It is
the Light in Darkness
we learn to know
slowly, like algebra.
It is Absence
as perfection,
the bride, the mother,
the one
who brushes lightly against you
with her wings.

SIMPLE

Now that summer has come,
you wear again the colors of summer.

Leaves scribble in air,
birdsong hides in light,

the scent of lilacs
trails like the hair of a girl.

Even at seventy it is remarkable! . . .
No surprise!

So it has always been.
You fill the eyes,

delightful any time,
wearing the colors of summer.

THE BLOOD OF THE ROSE

The blood of the rose
Is all the blood the rosebud knows.
Brightness falls from the air,
Holding darkness in its sphere.
Thorns with their sharp pricks
Are archetype of all cicatrix,
Soft throat, gentle voice
Lend occasion to rejoice,
Sweet gesture, sober face
Offer what we know of grace,
The garden and the garden gate
(Which we must negotiate)
Display the simple bending rose,
Upon whose tip the red blood flows.

I know we all mythologize our women

I know we all mythologize our women,
As cooks concoct new sauces in a kitchen;
We cannot see the simple walking creatures,
To whom we lend long legs and brilliant features;
And yet the truth is that the truth's best seen
Askance, so that the gilded soup tureen
Decked out with sauce and spice, is not less true
Than rancid meat, or yesterday's cold stew.

FAST

Her flame of hair flew backward on the wind.
Her laughter, too, out of her rippled throat.
The winds had never heard a clearer note
Freer than that she offered. She left behind
Laughter as sharp as scent, and as she passed
It whirled away in time's rough passing wind
Like incense or like smoke—though not like mind,
Which holds you like a vice, riveted fast.
Thus that evanescence was held too
Against the quick of time, as to a mast
A sail is fastened, held from winds' harass—
As if all passing were itself untrue!

As if her passing was itself the mast
To which her voice and flaming hair held fast.

MY SISTER, LIFE
—Pasternak

My Sister, Life! What passions we have known!
What arpeggios of sound, and what desire!
What liquid in the throat, what parching fire—
And all of it a gift—all of it *thrown!*
What orient warmth has harbored in our arms
As if one held a cat, a girl, a child;
What noises and what voices—and what wild
Cacophony of shouting and alarms!
What nights that pinned us, clasped by love or fear,
Or both together, tangled in that net
Where one lies frozen and yet drenched in sweat,
When love or hate or passion pins us near!

O, my Darling, O, my Sister, Life!
We're bound as close as two planks in a vice!

WIVES

What image swimming in the deep-blue sea
Rises from the sea in glistering light?
What creature of what depths, what fresh delight
Offers her fleshly beauty, offers her hair?
Wizard beauty, beauty to excite
The livelong day that is our daily light,
From setting forth to coming of the night,
From birth unto the light of last repair.

This narrative is told and then retold,
Because the telling can't discharge the need,
As waters spill the tank, or as the seed
Gives birth to other seed in manifold
Progression, recession, obsession;
The urge to love, which is the urge to be,
Or not to be, have it either way,
As from great height one sights the endless sea.

Seen from such height, it can go either way,
Dividing what might be from what might seem,
The weights are weighed upon the waiting beam
By that sharp fate that's sharper than a knife;
While dreadnaughts drag the ocean, and the girls
Are dragged from out the water soaking wet,
Their mermaid hair now tangled in the net,
And every sailor gets one as a wife.

MEXICO

The bang bang of the firecracker,
The howl of a dog,
The tarantula you killed in your bedroom . . .

Each day its revelation:
Seaweed choking the beach,
Children the color of milk-coffee,

The frigate bird
Balanced high-flying—
Poetry everywhere,

Panned from silt!
What difference does it make?—
This or that,

Manhattan or Mexico . . .
What difference except
Poetry! The universal

Shining in the particular,
The simplest words
Speaking our human need.

DIRECTION

If the answer were the ascending sky,
The birds themselves would teach us how to fly.

Depth must teach the ligament and knee
The lesson of its hard won liberty.

Dark defines the breadth as well as height
In whose high archingness the light can light.

Bodies instruct a man so he can learn
Direction, and the way in which to turn.

Words define the Poem and the World,
By which alone direction is inferred.

TRANSCENDENCE

i

The clouds that pass in the sky
Are sentences we cannot comprehend;

ii

And the dead children
Are holes in the universe; while the birds

iii

Fly upward under the sights of the gun . . .
Sing now the song of transcendence

iv

Like a man dying in a ditch,
Who sees in that immediacy

v

The fading heavens in his sight
Tower in the ever-lasting.

FALLING

As you would cling to your daughter when
She's falling, so he had clung to her—until
He had to let go . . . You saw the winter fill
Evening with its brassy fire, and now again
Snow is falling, and coldness bears the name
Of absence, absence, and the kingdom-come
Of thought, of need, is ice, and burdensome
As dread, though nothing is changed—all is the same
As when the ice-air fell like scalding rain,
Bitter as fire to human hearts, yes, because
Of its bad strength, which always was
Truth's awful force—which burned you up like flame!
O, fair she was, and falling—passing and fair,
And broke your verse against the granite air!

CLIMB!

Summer was over, and the summer birds
had flown away, and soon

autumn would burn its pyre. It was
his seventieth year to heaven,

he hunkered down, alone, afraid,
without instruction, without aid

against the insistent fact
of here-we-are! . . . Climb!

out of the air, into the sphere
where birds have flown, and flowers gone,

and leaves, like smoke, have blown—
although the blue remain, though not

the blue of summer days,
so easy in their ways, but like

the coming age of ice . . . Climb!
until the tears, the tears,

not from the years, but from
the wind, the wind that blows,

will speak!—Climb!

BOOK FIVE

THE CALLING

As the Sirens
called to Ulysses
(and their hair
twisted about them
in lightest brightness),
these images
crowd the page:
this way of saying,
these things
you came to say . . .

Step now into the sun,
where traffic blares,
the labyrinth of ways
astray in mid-direction,
noises,
women's voices,
letters,
lost questions,
misplaced expectations,
women, children,

infants
traveling
in fear and trembling
down corridors
into
the light—
the beat and heat

of
love—

inadequate love.

My father, my dear dead

My father, my dear dead!
why do you return to me now?
beneficent angel, unexpected guest,
more palpable than any ghost—
mere ghostly you! what
do you come to say, lost,
dearest man?—That all
shall be well? . . .

     Spirits
hover about us
with breath to show the way—
those
who have gone before,
like shafts of light
into the dark,
the fractured deep—and yet
remain
to skim us near,
weaving, leaving
within the ear
the heard,
the echoing voice.

FOR GABRIEL ON HIS SIXTEENTH BIRTHDAY

As sun falls scintillant on the ocean, spurring life,
So you, my shining grandson, spark and flash
The life of love in all of us, forever!

IF I DECLARE

If I declare that God is Love
It is the poem that knows what of
It's speaking, not the mortal man,
Whose life is but the average span
Of nonsense and absurdities,
Not equal to such words as these
I set down here, which I inferred,
Not from myself, but from the Word.

TO THE LIGHTHOUSE

In Virginia Woolf's great novel,
Light passes down walls, off waves,
Out of Lily Briscoe's painting.

Such is the nature of the eternal
Counted in the mensuration of the actual,
The palpable pulses of time. It is

A heart in which we live, a home,
A chamber in the breast,
A warm muscle of birth and dying.

We move within its music, and its chords
Compose our daily life, our living hours
Of breath and presence and visibility.

Its pulse is not the pulse of regnant Time,
The incommensurate, the overarching
Diaphragm of the that-which-is,

But short time's fleeting measurement,
Incarnate passingness, the human form
Of what we see and love. We dwell

Within the circulation of its blood,
The breathing world, as you might hold
A trembling dove between your hands.

It is an aging woman who lies down
To be caressed, having herself once been
Young and beautiful, who now is

Beautiful and old. Such are
The transformations of fleet time, which lend
Time's lineaments the inspiration of

The actual, like evening light
Falling across a wall. Its vagrant susurrations
Count the counterpoint of time's transfigurations,

The time in which we all can have
Our being and our home, the time in which
Mrs. Ramsey knits and loves and dies . . . .

Never believe it is immortal. It is
Our human isthmus, our peopled isle,
The sinuous echoing sounds like those

That echo in the flickering sonogram.
Time's length is time's short distance
Written across a lawn, its countless beams

Whose tom-tom-beats beat out the murmured step
Of passing time of all our days and ways, and so
Within the sober moments of duress

Count out the strokes of human passingness,
Within whose dark and certain stillness,
Death itself shall pass, shall surely pass.

A RING A JEWEL A POT OF GOLD

A ring, a jewel, a pot of gold ... two girls ...
Let's try again. A word, a verb, a rhyme;
A spinning wheel, a clock, brief fleeting time,
Which will not come again, though daylight whirls
About its axis in its whirligig,
Fast-motion: its swift and sure retreat
Into the gulf. So time will not repeat
Even this apple, this small pear, this fig
Hanging upon its stem ... much less a carnival
Of girls, of children, of onetime fatherhood
Clutched as your own, the zenith where you stood,
Sunlight, spring, the bursting comet's coronal ...

A ring, a jewel, a pot of gold, two girls,
A wave that rises and then, cresting, falls.

BE AT EASE, BE SURE

Be at ease, be sure, because
The bird's swift wing, the dove's,
Cuts the garden close,
Rising as light does.

But the shape of fear
Spreads from ear to ear
Frozen above our chin
Like a rictus grin.

Time won't let us pass,
Although we stop, we ask
Entrance, the right way—
But the foot's astray,

And the waters and
The blown and mounding sand
Rise to either side
And stop us—though the wide

Highway of the air
Flashes, and the sun
Urges us to come,
Beckoning—if we dare

Be at ease, be sure,
Because the soaring dove,
Rising far above
The garden, cuts the air.

LIKE CATTLE IN A FIELD

Slowly,
like cattle in a field,
you lift your head,

you see
wind in a tree,
roads

running away,
time's waste,
time's worry—

a confusion,
a mystery;
hear

water
underground,
music playing

all around,
wind that bloweth
where it listeth . . .

Confusion besets
the mind the eye—
the living and the dead

under grass,
here, where cows pass . . .
Close your mouth,

look north look south
up, down,
but no sound

can you utter,
only perhaps
a dumb mutter

as the cows do,
or rather a low moo
to express

their cow confusion.
You too
give a metaphysic moo

at field, at sky,
at clouds
as they go by.

MOTETS

i
the frogs by the roadside kept croaking
their desire, eructating love
beneath the weight of necessity,
the yoke and burden of our perennial need.

ii
Always
the ocean flows
around us, we sail
through blue eternity,
like earth
in the great picture
by di Paolo,
at the Metropolitan.

iii
The grandson was lost, but
down the aisle he ran,

crying,
Grandma, Grandma!

iv
blood
at the tip of a leaf

the headlong leap
through the flame

the praying mantis
motionless

on its stalk—
how many years ago?

       v
There was a man
who loved all manner of women and children,
so who could say
he did not love humanity?

       vi
Thunder in sunlight...
                Surely
even the stones
shining in air
are not more astounding,

more worthy of praise!

ANY DEITY

Betrayed again each day by his own body,
He leaned against a wall and spat a prayer
Between his teeth, the merest la-de-da-de
To his troubled mind, although the heart knows where
And whence such things get heard. Let the wind
Carry it off as offering, if it will,
To any god or deity it find
Who bothers with such matters, or who still
Attends to human frailty; for our kind
Is subject to the weakness of the flesh,
In fleshly matters, as in heart and mind,
Which send their spindle wishes for redress
As fervently as when the species was
Banished from Eden, and first knew distress.

IF YOU COME THIS FAR

If you come this far,
if you travel this distance,
if you follow any road
in any direction,
at any hour or day,
you will arrive at a different place—
not the one you chose,
nor any road you might have chosen,
but the place you earned
by coming this far—
a place without a *tu*, without a *s'il vous plaît*,
without a *Danke schön*; a place
of truth—a sort of truth,
crooked but true, a
part and parcel of your being you,
the people you knew, the faces
changed but true, altered
according to a law—
the fact of having come this far ...
You thought to avoid
these misconceptions—imagining
what? On what evidence? ... But
you won't turn back, won't
return your ticket—although
it is a joke at which one merely smiles,
with people in cheap clothes,
sequinned dresses,
bathing suits too tight
too loud too bare ... yes,

it is a misunderstanding, like
mud and moonshine . . . You
have traveled this far, in one weather
or another, coming this distance,
following this road, enjoying
this company . . . although
it is a place you hadn't anticipated,
never expected or foresaw: the
exiguous conclusion of love . . .
                              And yet,
and yet . . . if you persisted,
if you continued beyond
this strange purlieu,
this termination, this other direction,
you would reach
another destination,
a different location,
le temps retrouvé, let's say . . . If you
continued (and it might be
for no more than an instant!)
you would find
the places,
the remembered faces,
sunlight on the grass,
the hours and days that passed,
the children playing,
the voices saying
the things you remember,
the small hands offered,
the hands, the hands!—
the promised destination.

Luminous, the flowers shine in light

Luminous, the flowers shine in light
Within fast day's now certain slow decline.
They are small flames, but only to such sight
As sees them so, as the shades refine

The greens and grays into the gathering night.
It gathers in the mystery of the darkness,
The darkness that in dark reveals the light,
Revealing light by means of its own darkness.

And the hedge, the long gray grass, the leaves
Collect the dark light as a watch its time,
So that in darkness brightness still may shine,
Like light on ocean after the sunlight leaves.

But now the light of green turns purple-gray
As water's blue turns slowly to opaque,
And what the eye beholds for darkness' sake
Is light gone down to darkness for the day.

NOW THE BREATH OF THE WOMAN YOU LOVE

Now the breath of the woman you love
returns from half a century. Touch
the pulse of time—touch

the skin of peach-like softness.
Whatever is lost, whatever forgotten,
remains in some undisclosed location

untouched, unclaimed, as on the ocean floor
the keel of a ship. Behold your life
held up to the sun—time in eternity!

The odor of sweetbriar, the odor
of rooms now closed forever,
the scent from half a century distant—

the breath of the woman you love.

TITIAN WOULD HAVE PAINTED HER

Titian would have painted her,
Giorgione, when they were young,
when *she* was young. The shape of the thigh,
the shape of the breast, the shape
of her reclining splendor.
                      If you reached out,
you would touch a hand, an arm,
a curtain blowing . . .
                      We stutter
to say the universal, although
it is the particular we love.

Darkness blots the eye, a light
too bright for seeing . . . Why
do we cry out as if it mattered, as if
any of it mattered?—summer
repeats itself
like an irrational number . . . And yet
we are not repeated.

August squanders the sun.
Paint cracks on the canvas.

The classic lines return
again, again,
the shape of the leg,
the shape of the brow,
the shape of the human:
       the familiar . . .
                the unrepeatable.

DIVINING

Love leads the eye to love what is divine;
So Plato thought, and so the poets have sung
In English verse or sweet Italian,
Speaking of women and the feminine
Incarnation of their graceful being.
It is not flesh alone, but revelation of
The transubstantiated fact of love,
Which moves in sway of line, so that our seeing
Is revelation of the brief divine
Embodied in that falling that we are,
Refracted like pure light, but insofar
As light in all its color will make shine

The intimation of that other light,
Which is all color recombined in white.

UPON THE EARTH

i

Love inhabited every corner of her body,
from nighttime to the crowning of day,
from crying (O, too much crying!)
to learning not to cry. It inhabited
the fancy dresses, twirled like leaves
in childhood; in adolescence;
in the outgrowing of adolescence
like a pair of shoes outgrown. It moved
on legs that were flawless, moved
in the beating of her heart, her mind
measuring, judging, rejecting... It lived
along the wrists, the tapering ankles,
the well-shaped calves... Love dwelt
in every corner, in her setting forth
like a dancer, onto the brittle glass ceiling
of the world...

ii

Was she not like a marvelous sloop
glancing over water? Graceful,
sturdy, beautiful... like
a dancer twirling... But
the pattern had been cut
by hands that were inadequate,
for she came from a different cloth,
another mold, irreplaceable,
unrepeatable—her own.

iii

Bend like a tree
to its own reflection. Be
the strait-grained lines
of Shaker furniture. Be
the Delftware
glorying in mastery. Be
the voice that answers
to your questioning . . . Be!

iv

Why
did God bend down
out of Heaven
to create the world? Why,
from a breath, a bone,
a rib, the particular,
the peculiar,
harbored
once only,
the irreplaceable,
the loved one,
the disappearing—here,
on earth,
this time only?

Because the loveliness of all this world

Because the loveliness of all this world
Is not enough... And so it can't fill up
One's emptiness, as if the half-filled cup
Remained half empty, though the waters pearled
Over the edge... Item, the sound of rain
Pattering on leaves. Item, the dappled drops
Shining in autumn weather; item, the treetops
Glittering in sun; the scent of long-lost Maine.
Here is depth that leaves behind the ache
For that which was—the amputated limb,
Time's corridor where time fills to the brim
With emptiness, for dearest absence's sake:

The cry for substance where once substance was,
The fading fragrance of the now-blown rose.

THE STAGE

This is the place that is and always was
The World. It stretches about you for about
One mile—the distance you can always see,
The space that moves with you and always has,
The center of your stage. So here you stand,
Repeating your lines, the Hero (if you will),
Or just yourself, your mother's son, set out
This very day to see what you can see,
The tale they promised you. Yes, here you are
Dead center. The village idiot drools;
The stony tower rises by the road;
The chopping block is here; the maiden with her hair...
So there you stand quite lost—and yet, and yet...
Dead center on the only stage there'll be.

LABYRINTH

This labyrinth, this riddle, this weird maze,
Never believe it does not have a center.
For though it's true that on the day you enter,
Its outer look may not command your gaze.
Most passers-by regard with casual eye
Its bland façade, noting with but a glance
The heretofore, the here, the happenstance,
Which earn no better than a curt reply
Of bored dismissal. But the surface is
No proper measure, fashioned to deceive
The passing stranger, and in short to leave
Its inner essence for dull eyes to miss.
And yet it's certain that its center is
Waiting, unfathomable—a bottomless abyss.

THE CIRCLE

The eye takes in the length from here to there,
A field, a hill, a breadth of brilliant sky,
Seen with the mind, seen with the accuracy
Of right insight. And so, no matter where
The circle moves, our seeing circle too
Moves there. The world we see moves in accord
With that same moving, and the eyes record
The one eternal sight of what is true
For *you*, the bourne of all your mortal seeing:
The City and the Garden and the Way
That is your own, in which your destiny
Unfolds, and thereby manifests your being.
And there within that circle stands the Tree
That marks forever your Centrality.

THE TRADITION

The book contains the tale they promised you.
For on the page there runs a narrow road,
A single lane scarce larger than a path
Crossing a field, twisting beneath a sky
Gray and empty as a dead man's stare.
The sun is harsh, it presses on your back
With its full weight, as of a prohibition.
You know the place, have read the book before—
The battlements with their crenelated tower,
The ravens circling slowly, and the horse
Grazing in the adjacent field . . . What tower? What horse?
What men exchanging words with sinister voices? . . .
Here is the field you have to cross, the well,
The village and the sturdy wooden stocks.
Take up the tale, take up the fabled stone
Which you alone can lift, the speaking shell,
The boat made out of linden wood that rides
Beside the splintered pier. You know the place,
The sentence, illustration, and the sign,
The axe, the swinging rope, the muttered voice,
The hero and the riddle and the girl
Waiting for you, waiting just for you—
The story that you always knew you knew.

SHORTS

i

Again the roses flout the sun,
And tulips shout as at a stadium
Where emperors come
To watch the gladiators kill for fun.

ii

The dark that moves in light
Assumes the cloak of night,
Until, the other way,
Sun redeems the day.

iii

Slowly the telegrams kept arriving
from the empty expanses of the sky.

iv

Up the Mountain of Death
He toiled with shortened breath,
Until the Mountain said
Traveler, try another way instead!

v

The borrowed image is not borrowed, for
You found it in your mind before
You met it on the page. Its reflection
Precedes the words that lent it recollection.

vi

The rose that bends above the thorn
Utters one word the whole day long,
Unmindful of the blood that's drawn
Out of the earth, to feed its song.

vii

The sun that says a single word
Is understood, although not heard,
Like the universal sound
The stars make as they swirl around.

viii

What explains our coming?—what the ground
Of our existence, what the strange compound
Of pleasure with its sure adjutant pain,
Which, in hope of love, will start again
The cycle of becoming, and the round
We gamely sing, as we go round and round
The spiral stair, which ends back at the start,
But higher up, along the twisting heart.

ix

Because of what he'd seen,
His last word would be green,
Although, it's also true,
It might as well be blue.

x

And at the tip of the rose its red unfurled,
As if it did not know another word.

Whatever time has done, I love you more

Whatever time has done, I love you more
(If such can be accounted more or less),
Not only for what you are, but (I confess)
For those dark scars that time inflicts, which score
Your lovely face—the sign of lasting pain,
Which is the writ of short time's testimony;
Love's countless failures, a sad inventory
Scripted in daily measure; the refrain
The years accumulate—time's testament
Of love, of passion, of our life together,
Whether for good, as I assert, or whether
One counts past time as one long slow lament.

The night comes on, and with the night the same
Darkness, where you hold your steady flame.

THE STAYING THINGS

As a young man he wrote his young man's poems
To celebrate the body's love and seasons;
For these display their own sufficient reasons
For being sung, and always will. Their wrongs

Or rights are equal to such song, and so
Deserve their singing and their celebration;
For verse is fit for youth's exhilaration
And momentary joy. Otherwise, we grow

In time to our inheritance—which is
True singing in its ancient lineaments,
Which tell of these things in their permanence,
As singing knows: the shape of what exists

Before and after: not just the everyday
In all its everyday confusion, but
The common day transfigured, so it's not
Merely the babbling of what we say

In all our dull and daily passingness
 (The Jack who woke and brushed his teeth and yawned):
All of the squiggling things that Being spawned
Only to throw away. But we express

The Road we travelled, and the Bread we ate,
The Rose that pierced the eye and hurt the hand,
Love and Death and Sorrow, and the Land
We loved and left—until our poems repeat,

By right analogy, spoken in words that stay,
The staying things upon their passing way.

ALWAYS A GIRL

No girl, you tell me. But to me, always
A girl—who loved you as a girl! The years
Can only heap deception. What appears
In body or in face—whose malversation frays
That knowledge, that right image—countervenes
The speaking truth of what you still remain.
But if there now are wrinkles, time's dark stain
Of years—accumulation that now seems
To darken time's true lineaments—they serve
Only to make more dear that dearest thing
You are, remain. So I assert that nothing
Can mar those lines, that gracious, graceful curve
That was the girl who still stands in my eye,
Giving the lie to swift time's ceaseless lie.

This ecstasy, this long drawn otherness

This ecstasy, this long drawn otherness,
Why is it not the common grass that grows
Beside the wall? This sound, this touch, this taste,

This fine repletion of the eye, the willing tongue,
This brimful seeing of the light of day,
As if these things were flesh and butter, were

Words that make the signs that are the things
Transformed, as seasons are, as colors are,
By the imagination, at first sight.

I'm speaking soberly, as bird-talk is,
Which can but speak its need, like poetry,
Speaking the need that makes it speak the poem,

That makes it say the actual: thigh, ribcage, skull
Lying amid the grass in some small field
Where insects chug and chitter in the sun.

I want to say this fact, this otherness,
As in a world composed of flesh and bone,
Which is the case, the world we're speaking of,

The world of skin and blood and brooding death—
The death that holds dominion over all:
Mind, the thrust of mind, the need of mind,

The thrusting, needing mind of all of us,
The lost, the mortal, crying, needing voice,
A braying mule, a wailing new born child . . .

It is the cry of women in their need,
Laughter of playgrounds, raucous cough of men,
A rusty gate that swings, a swinging gate . . .

I wanted to say the world, and this I say
Not as the ocean does, or splintering tree,
Or biting fire, or cold, but as the wind

That leans against a wall, a crumbling wall,
A skull of fox or crow, a glacial scree,
An upright boulder, a bare and wind-swept hill.

Photo copyright © 2021 Ronnie Ann Herman

John Herman grew up in the outskirts of New York City. He received a Doctorate in English Literature from the University of California at Berkeley, and has taught at the Sorbonne (*Paris IV*), and the University of Massachusetts in Boston. He then worked in Manhattan as an editor, first at Simon and Schuster, then as the Editorial Director of Weidenfeld & Nicolson, and then of Ticknor & Fields, a division of Houghton Mifflin. For fifteen years he was the Associate Director of the Graduate Writing Program at Manhattanville College in Purchase, New York.

As well as a previous book of poetry, *White Summer* (EternEditions), Herman has published four novels, *The Weight of Love* (selected by *Publishers Weekly* as one of the best novels of the year), and *The Light of Common Day* (both Nan Talese Books), as well as *Deep Waters* and *Labyrinth* (both Philomel Books). Mr. Herman lives with his wife in New York City and upstate New York. They have two daughters and six grandchildren.

www.ingramcontent.com/pod-product-compliance
Lightning Source LLC
Chambersburg PA
CBHW031631160426
43196CB00006B/366